To You and family,

May God bless you

throughout

all the seasons of your lives.

Laurie Bohler

11/13/01

Prayers *through* *the* Seasons

Previous page - Roadside wildflowers, Texas

Opposite page - Roaring brook, Vermont

Highlands, Costa Rica

Prayers *through* *the* Seasons

An inspirational collection of Christian prayers and nature photography

Reverend Deborah Kaiser-Cross

Photography by David Middleton

Foreword by Dr. Barry Johnson

Created by Laurie Bohlke

Radiant
River Press

St. Charles, Illinois

Publisher's Cataloging-in-Publication
(Provided by Quality Books, Inc.)

Kaiser-Cross, Deborah.
  Prayers through the seasons : an inspirational
collection of Christian prayers and nature photography /
Deborah Kaiser-Cross ; photography by David Middleton ;
foreword by Barry Johnson ; created by Laurie Bohlke. --
1st ed.
  p. cm.
  Includes index.
  LCCN 2001117403
  ISBN 0-9711020-0-7

  1. Prayers. 2. Nature--Pictorial works.
I. Middleton, David, 1955- II. Title.

BV245.K45 2001   242'.8
                QBI01-700722

Edited by Laurie Bohlke
Book design: Paetzold Associates, Jennifer Lund, designer
Printed in China by Everbest Printing Co, Ltd. through Four Colour Imports, Ltd.

The colors in this book have been matched as closely as possible to the original 35mm slides. The colors have not been digitally enhanced or altered.

Cade's Cove, Great Smoky Mountains National Park, Tennessee

For my husband David, the strength of my heart.

For Anne, Sarah, and Michael, the joy of my life.

Deborah Kaiser-Cross

King penguins, South Georgia Island

I am deeply appreciative for the many friends who encouraged me in the writing of this book:

For Laurie Bohlke who served as a most able and exacting editor. She made my simple musings sound so much richer. I am even more grateful for her constant inspiration and compelling vision that brought this book to completion.

For David Middleton whose photography brings life and depth to the offerings of my heart.

For all the pastors, poets, and psalmists who have touched my life with prayers rich in visual imagery. For each who opened my eyes to all the gifts surrounding me and beckoned me to Abba, Father.

For Dr. Barry Johnson and Barbara Johnson who have graced me with their friendship.

For JupiterFIRST Church staff and congregation who have blessed me with their affirmation in this project.

For my parents, Charles and Rosemary Cross, whose belief in me began this joyful journey.

Most of all, I am grateful for my husband, David, and his unfailing love and encouragement. And for our children, Anne, Sarah, and Michael, who have supported me in the time that this book took away from them. My life is full because of you!

Deborah Kaiser-Cross

In creating and developing this book, I tackled a project that appeared like a tiny iceberg floating in a large sea of creative possibility. Month by month, more of the iceberg heaved out of the tumultuous sea until even my infamous list making abilities were strained. But I felt absolutely compelled to honor God and his glorious world with this book.

So many people stepped forward to help me. First, very special thanks to Deb and David for their talent, perseverance and patience in dealing with my ever-present e-mails and deadlines. Deb's gentle soul, her radiant spirituality, and her friendship have inspired all my efforts. David has been my erudite mentor throughout the entire book project, patiently discussing all my major issues and my minor questions.

I am so grateful to Dr. Barry Johnson for writing the foreword and offering his expertise during the book's development.

Thanks to my friend, Mary Carol Smith, who conceptualized the initial graphic design with me. Bill Paetzold of Paetzold Associates and his group, particularly Jennifer Lund, were outstanding in providing the final graphic design for the book.

My cadre of discerning readers was so instrumental in polishing the text. Thanks to Bill Bohlke, Leanne Flusser, Margaret Kelly, Barbara Johnson, Patricia Kitner, Susan Klipp, David Middleton, Reverend John Rodgers and Mary Carol Smith. Barbara Kuebler and Wayne Lynch, both talented photographers, have generously shared images of Deb and David for the back flap of the dust jacket.

Photographers Chris Harris and Chuck Veatch, Jim Galvin of Livingstone Corporation, Eric Anderson of Illinois Graphics, Mike McCoy of Jostens Commercial Publications and Eric Taylor of Four Colour Imports graciously shared their expertise about printing and publishing.

Many thanks to my patient proofreading team of Claire Beck, Bill Bohlke, Barbara Johnson, Deb Kaiser-Cross, David Middleton, Kristen and Doug Natelson and Gail Perkins. Finally, thanks and love to my always-supportive family, especially Kristen, Doug, Kevin, and my husband, Bill.

Laurie Bohlke

Table of Contents

Dwarf iris, Tennessee

Western sunflower, Colorado

Hackleman Grove, Cascade Mountains, Oregon

Red maples, Maine

Saguaro with lupine and Mexican gold poppies, Arizona

Foreword

Years ago, while serving as Senior Minister of Shiloh Church in Dayton, Ohio, I decided to spruce up my office with a live plant. The lady at the greenhouse told me my best bet would be a schefflera. "They're big, they're beautiful and they don't require much attention. Just water and enjoy!" So I purchased this glorious plant, about four feet tall, in a quaint wooden pot perched on a three-legged pedestal. I couldn't believe the response of the office secretaries when I came through the door toting my treasure. It was like taking a puppy to the beach. "Oh, look at that. What a beautiful plant! We didn't know you had a green thumb. How sweet."

Carefully, I located my life's horticultural high-point in the corner of my office.

Less than a week later, I was working at my desk when I heard a muffled thump. The schefflera was flat on the floor. Not thinking much about it, I stood it up and went back to work. Two days later, "Whump!" Same thing. After four or five such episodes, I humbly sought the assistance of my secretary. She took one look, noted how the plant had fallen toward the window and summed up my problem. "You have to turn it, silly. It's reaching for the sun!"

Whenever I dwell on prayer, my thoughts return to that incident. You see, I believe it is not only natural but extremely healthy for all of us to "reach for the sun!" To reach for nourishment and strength, to open ourselves to fresh energy and deeper understanding, to posture our heads and hearts to receive God's blessings and God's guidance, as both are perpetually dispensed all around us. Of course, all the while we need to keep turning, expanding the horizons of our percipience, widening our range of vision and sensitivity so as to fully absorb our Heavenly Creator's timeless love.

Some people are better at it than others. Deborah Kaiser-Cross is one of those. For the past eight years I have had the privilege of hearing and reading her prayers. Time after time, they have lifted me to a fresh level of appreciation for what God has done and is doing in my life. She just has that knack...an almost extra-sensory perception for sensing the divine...for spotting the Creator's fingerprints. Not only in the big, predictable areas like majestic mountain ranges, but also in the little stuff like the intricacies of a baby's hand or the blurred efficiency of a hummingbird's wing. This alone makes her prayers a delight to the senses. But that's not all. Deb's prayers bring something else that is very special to all of us who feed on them. I don't know how, but somehow her prayers invite us to change. To reconsider. To drop old biases and embrace new possibilities. To fully participate in the dance of life. To grow.

Were this book but a printed collection of Deb's prayers, its value would outrun the years undoubtedly destined to yellow its pages.

It is more.

Enter the genius of David Middleton.

I believe it was the popular singer, the late Jim Croce, who once observed, "Some people feel the rain, others just get wet!" David Middleton feels the rain. From the first time I saw one of his photographs, I knew this man was gifted. It was a picture of a display of hats, women's hats, straw hats, colorful hats. Had I been passing the actual display, I suppose it might have caught my eye simply because it was so colorful. David's photograph takes one a lot further than that. It seems to summon the viewer to consider a choice...and through the choice the nature of the chooser. A wonderful reminder that every human being is a unique and unrepeatable miracle of God. All this...through a photograph of a collection of hats. Dwelling on such talent it comes to me that even the most common among us has some sensitivity to the exceptional. We know when we hear a stirring piece of music, or witness a spectacular sunrise, or behold the majesty of the ocean when it is angry. But very few of us have the capacity to transform the ordinary into the extraordinary. Like Middleton did with those hats. The good news? As you will see in these pages, he does it all the time. Routinely. With the flick of a lens this guy stretches the boundaries of the mind and the fence lines of the soul welcoming us to see and consider depth, meaning, beauty and strength heretofore overlooked.

Again, as a collection on its own, these David Middleton photographs are a treasure.

Blended with the prayers of Deborah Kaiser-Cross, the result is profound.

My prayer? That you might use this book to reach for the sun...and find Him!

Barry L. Johnson
Senior Minister, JupiterFIRST Church

Jimsonweed, California

Preface

Larkspur, Colorado

How to be "the best" at something? I don't know, but I do know that Reverend Deborah Kaiser-Cross gives the best prayers that I have ever heard. Week after week, month after month, she holds the congregation of JupiterFIRST Church spellbound with her lyrical, spiritually uplifting prayers.

Five years ago, the evocative nature references included in many of Deb's prayers gave me an idea. My brother, David Middleton, is a gifted professional nature photographer. His spectacular photographs combined with her heartfelt prayers would create an inspirational book.

Prayers through the Seasons' fifty-three prayers are organized by seasons, with thirteen prayers in each season and a closing prayer. You may want to read the book straight through or read a prayer a week, but you could also simply open the book at random and join Deb in prayer. Enjoy nature's beauty as you open your soul to God.

Many of the prayers were born out of images or verses from the Scripture. In the biblical notes on pages 136-137, we have listed each biblical reference. You may want to use these to enhance your reading of these prayers.

My prayer would be that this book would bring readers closer to God and their faith, helping them through all the seasons of their lives.

Laurie Bohlke

This book was born out of a love relationship between a pastor and a remarkable congregation. Sunday after Sunday, I am blessed to be able to serve as Minister of Pastoral Care and Counseling at JupiterFIRST Church in Jupiter, Florida. During each service of worship, I fashion a prayer that comes from my life experienced with this community of faith in that particular week. The prayers that you find in this book were originally written for this worshiping congregation. Our shared laughter and joy, tears and tragedy, all find their home in our prayer time together. As the prayers made their way from a worship setting into book form, they were changed into the first person, so that they might resonate with the life of each person picking up this book.

Laurie and I struggled to find a way to deal with gender neutrality, an ongoing church issue, in this book. I wanted to remain true to my prayers which have always included biblical references to God as Lord, Abba and Father. So we decided to increase the number of gender neutral salutations. However, please use any salutation that brings you closer to God.

For many of us, Sunday worship is sacred time. It is a time set aside to be still and ponder the majesty of God, to seek that quiet place where we can dwell with the Lord, and to know our souls have been restored by his still waters. This book was created out of my hope that sacred time might be transformed to any time we seek the Lord. It is my heartfelt prayer that you might pick up this book and discover that sacred time.

I pray that you might appreciate anew the grandeur of the created order, that you might know his peace that passes all understanding, and sense the pulse of God reaching out to you in the person of Jesus Christ. My simple hope is that the musings from my heart to the Lord might now minister to your heart as well.

Deborah Kaiser-Cross

Saint John's wort, Vermont

As a professional nature photographer, I have spent years trying to capture the beauty of the natural world on film. Traveling half the year and shooting 500 rolls of film a year, I have amassed a library of over 100,000 images. I have had the good fortune to film great gatherings of bears, birds and butterflies; I have shot portraits of owls, tigers and wildflowers; and I have photographed sweeping landscapes of forests, canyons, and seacoasts. In pursuit of the image, I have crawled through penguin colonies, wandered through ancient forests, stomped through snowy meadows, sweated through rainforests, and climbed alpine ridges. I have gone everywhere to photograph everything.

And yet as rewarding as it is to get the shot and go where I have been, there was always something missing when the pursuit and capture were complete. A photograph can preserve a moment in time but not the emotion being felt at that time. Awe and reverence are fleeting no matter what kind of film is used. This is why I enjoyed participating in the development of this book. The prayers add layers of wonder and spirituality to the photographs.

A note to photographers: Every one of these images was taken with standard 35mm camera equipment. No filtering was done to enhance color and no digital manipulation was used to alter any of the pictures. I feel it is better to wait for the magic to appear than to artificially create it from something that was not there.

David Middleton

Moraine Lake, Banff National Park, Alberta, Canada

Spring

Black bear cub, Montana

Little Pigeon River, Great Smoky Mountains National Park, Tennessee

O Prince of Peace, who rejoiced in the

early sun rising over the misty shores of the

Sea of Galilee, may my day begin as yours

so often did—in the quiet faithfulness of

whispered prayer.

Dogwood blossoms, Tennessee

Previous pages - Mt. Moran, Grand Teton National Park, Wyoming

*S*pirit of the living God, in this season that celebrates new beginnings, come and be the gardener of my soul. I invite you to prune away the withered branches of my life, to till the soil of my soul until the seeds of creation burst forth and blossom.

Bunchberry flowers, Oregon

Cade's Cove sunrise, Great Smoky Mountains National Park, Tennessee

Glorious God, out of nothingness you fashioned this world of beauty. Thank you for the joy of witnessing the ever-changing rainbow hues of the dawning sky. I treasure the bright spring sunshine illuminating the green of growing grass and glinting on thawed rivers and lakes. As colorful flowers emerge from their winter slumber, I feel renewed and ready to go forth into the world, trusting in you to lead the way.

Calypso orchids, Colorado

Horse farm, Lexington, Kentucky

*G*od of all seasons, even as I thank you for the extraordinary,

precious gift of life itself, I regret how quickly time seems to

slip away from me. Immersed in yesterday's events and

tomorrow's dreams, I often pass by today's hidden pleasures.

Open my eyes to see your hand in each moment, each

encounter, and each person who touches my life today.

Mother and foal, Lexington, Kentucky

Springtime Sonoran desert, Arizona

*L*ord, remind me again that the more I depend on you,

the more concerns I entrust to your care, the more room

you have to work in my life, surprising me with your goodness.

Desert poppies and saguro, Arizona

*S*urprise me, O God! Surprise me with your gift of hope and peace. Help me to look up—to laugh and sing. You are the One who can make light shine in the midst of darkness. You turn sorrow into song and mourning into joy—through Jesus whose victory over sin and death is the source of all my faith.

Daffodil fields, Skagit Valley, Washington

Previous pages - Peggy's Cove lighthouse, Nova Scotia, Canada

Amazing God, I offer you my gratitude for all the gifts of unexpected grace that touch my life. The abundant rainfall illustrates your cleansing forgiveness poured out upon my heart. The budding sprouts of spring remind me that each morning you are recreating me anew in the image of Jesus Christ. The eternal rhythm of each day, from spectacular sunrise to soaring sunset, signals your unfailing presence sustaining my soul. O God, I long to be filled with the freshness of your living love. Come and bless me with your presence.

Colorado columbine, Colorado

Hooker's fairy bell, California

Gentle God, like the disciples in the upper room, I wait for your

Spirit's touch. Help me to be still as I listen for your Word speaking in

my quieted heart. I want to know that you are here with me always.

Yellow trillium, North Carolina

Avalanche lilies, Washington (both)

Gracious God, on this glorious Easter morning, all your handiwork joins in creation's chorus of celebration. I rejoice in the warmth of the sunshine streaming through my soul. Thank you for the delight of spring blossoms scenting the air, for the melody of songbirds, and for the engaging laughter of children. On this day of days, with such beauty surrounding me, I gladly turn to you with praise and thanksgiving.

O risen Lord, I am privileged to sit at your nail-scarred feet, beholding your love. I pray that you will roll away the gravestone from those circumstances that shroud my heart and entomb my soul. Where there is guilt, chase away the night with your healing forgiveness. Where there is worry, lift the stone of fear and resurrect my courage. Where there is sadness, cast aside the grave clothes and release my joy.

O living Christ, in each troubled place on this earth, I pray that you will bring the dawn of new hope. Capture me with the power of the resurrection that I might seek new life in you.

Highland children, Ecuador

Dear God, I am reminded that you have called each of us to live within families. Thank you for the wisdom of older persons who link me with the past, enriching me with their experience. Thank you for children, so rich in potential, growing up before my eyes.

Wonderful Counselor, I invite you to enter my home, not as an occupant of a guestroom, but as the senior member of the household. Enable me to personify your love in the most ordinary parts of my life. Keep me human as you make me holy.

Settler's cabin, Tennessee

O God, just when my life becomes comfortable, you bring forth a new challenge.

When a situation becomes impossible, you move to create a fresh possibility. When

so much of my soul seems to be dying on the inside, you cause blossoms of hope

to sprout. When my heart becomes hardened, you embrace my fears, melting my

defenses. O God of grace, help me to trust you at work, changing me into the

likeness of your Son, Jesus Christ.

Cinnamon fern fiddlehead, Vermont

*L*ord, remind me again that the more I

depend on you, the more concerns I entrust

to your care, the more room you have to work

in my life, surprising me with your goodness.

Hedgehodge cactus, Arizona

Prickly-pear cacti and flowers, Arizona

*U*se me, O God. Send me along the

road with Christ. Let the wind blow

in my face and the sun shine in my

valley. Send me out along the highways

of the heart. Let my hands be guided by

your hand and my steps by your steps.

Lord Jesus, help me to release my life

into your care, so that I might freely

and joyfully journey with you.

Emma's Creek, Vermont

Previous pages - Clearing storm on Hurricane Ridge, Olympic National Park, Washington

Summer

Short-eared owl, Wyoming

Thank you, Wondrous Creator, for the scampering play of squirrels among the pines, for the breathtaking loveliness of roses in full bloom, and for the perfect balance of the eagle's wings. I praise you, O Master Craftsman, for everything expertly fashioned by your hand.

*M*ost Holy God, you meet me in the dawning hours of each

new day, while the mists of morning float from the horizon.

Rays of sunlight touch me with healing warmth. The gentle

caress of a soft breeze awakens me to your presence.

O Lord, I come as a seeker of your heart. I yearn to know the

power of Jesus' presence—to hear his Word, to see his face.

Energize my mind and spirit, so that I might see Jesus Christ

in each person I meet.

Rhododendrons in old-growth forest, Oregon

Previous pages - Golden eagle, Colorado

Rhododendron blossoms, Oregon

Land iguana, Galapagos Islands, Ecuador

*E*verlasting Father, give me enough challenges to make me strong, enough reality

to know my weaknesses, and enough humility to know that I need your presence

daily. Bless me with the enduring, life-giving faith to know that your grace is

sufficient for me. You, O God, are the source of all my strength and hope.

Purple vetch, New Mexico

O God, simple, ordinary things so often bring joy. Leaves dancing in the noontime breeze, butterflies fluttering among fresh blossoms, fragrant pine boughs swaying in a summer storm—all delight my senses. As I watch children skipping barefoot in grass so green and see the sparkle of a smile lighting up a loved one's face, I praise and honor you, O great Creator.

Texas meadow, Hill Country, Texas

Ringlet butterfly, Vermont

Sunrise, Lexington, Kentucky

Desert primrose, California

O wondrous God, when sunshine dances across the cornflower sky, your glory shines through the heavens. As I bow in prayer before your majesty, inspire me to step back from the turbulence of these times to reflect on the direction of my life.

Mighty God, light the fires of your Holy Spirit in every fiber of my being. Open my mind to new possibilities so that I might make a difference in this needy world. I pray that my faith will strengthen me to serve others more boldly in the name of your Son, Jesus Christ.

Spring beauty flower, Wisconsin

Shepherd of my soul, who will not turn away anyone calling out in prayer, I reach out to take your outstretched hand. Hear my prayer, for I am your child, and like a child, I often lose my way. I need your forgiveness for the times when I have disappointed the ones who count on me. I remember deeds left undone and opportunities not taken. There have been many days when my anxiety has overwhelmed my trust in you. Wash over my heart with the gentle rain of your Holy Spirit and cleanse me with your forgiving grace.

Dewy spider web, Texas

*L*ord of the universe, I envision the magnificence of your created order. You have given constellations their form and shaped the majesty of mountain ranges. Yet, you have designed the grasp of a child's hand and intricately formed the span of a hummingbird's wing. Robins, rushing rivers and whistling winds echo your glorious song. The poetry of each flaming sunset inspires me to pause and thank you, O God, for creating your world with such exquisite complexity.

Summer cabin, Colorado

Previous pages - Palm sunset, Naples, Florida

64

O God of light, all of heaven and earth declares your glory in displays of your amazing handiwork. In the midst of an all too busy life, I pause for vacation and hear your whispered notes of refreshment and peace. The inviting splash of a mountain stream reminds me of your everlasting faithfulness. The sturdiness of the lofty redwood trees heralds your mighty power. The wispy ribbons of clouds inspire me to envision your divine paintbrush sweeping forgiveness into a penitent soul.

You have taught me that in returning and rest I shall be restored. In quietness and confidence I shall be strengthened. Lead me into your presence, where I might be still and know that you are God.

Yucca and flower, Texas

God of grace, help me to know from the depths of my being

that the circumstances in my life do not have to control me.

I trust you to lead me through them.

Lady beetle, Pennsylvania

*G*racious God, teach me to live daily with a grateful spirit,

reflecting often on the gifts you shower upon me. Before my

mind begins to envision the workday ahead, I celebrate the gift

of summer joys. Memories of roaring surf tickling my toes make

me grin as I picture children twirling, exuberantly free on a

deserted beach. Hiking rocky mountain paths contrasts with

lazy afternoons when I drink in the refreshment of your

renewing peace.

I remember the delight that comes with a child's rushing hug,

the tenderness that emanates from the eyes of aged loved ones,

and the warmth of friends, who love

me as I am. Let your peace embrace

me as I return to the demands of a

busy life.

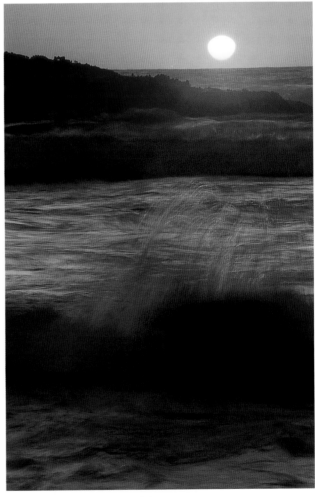

Hurricane Ridge, Olympic National Park, Washington

Sunset, redwood coast, California

*A*s I enter your presence, O God, I hesitate to pray for patience,

which only develops through times of testing and trial. Teach me

the secret of releasing my expectations so that my children might

discover the peace that dwells in the home of patient parents.

Thank you for the gift of family life, for I am discovering that

it is the sandpaper that you use to smooth out the rough edges of

my character. You offer me a perfect parent's love, unconditional,

faithful, and sure. Abba, may my heart discover the peace that

surpasses my understanding, the peace that comes from

abiding in you.

Gentoo penguin and chicks, Falkland Islands

Summer spider, Vermont

*W*onderful Counselor, I bring my heart's concerns to you today. I know that there are things that I must do and ask you for the strength and courage to do them. I know that there are things that confuse me. Grant me insight and wisdom in my decision making. Some things are simply out of my control, so I pray for the faith to let go and trust in you, O Lord.

Blacktail Pond and Grand Tetons, Grand Teton National Park, Wyoming

Twilight dory, Nova Scotia

*L*ord, bless me in my working and my relaxing, in my

loving and my laughing, that I might go forth this day joyful

and anchor-sure within. Capture my heart with the drama

and power of what you might do through me, in the name

of Jesus who guides my life.

Tidepool, Washington coast

Autumn

Milkweed pod, Vermont

Roaring brook, Vermont

Bobcat, near Kalispell, Montana

*G*lorious God, as the leafy green of summer gently flows into the brilliant hues of autumn's landscape, may your Spirit lead me boldly into a new season with you. Open the eyes of my soul that I might glimpse the subtle changes you are bringing forth in my own life. I am willing to follow where you lead, helping others to find strength in your daily presence.

Sugar maple, New Hampshire

O Lord, as another school year begins, bless those who guide our children. These busy people are patient and accepting, taking the time to listen and daring to walk with their students side by side.

Gentle God, be with our young ones always, reaching out to them with the power of Jesus Christ wherever they go. Help our youth to make a commitment of faith that will enable them to navigate a strong and steady course in the turbulent waters of our times.

Blood star on kelp, Washington

Surf at Boiler Bay, Oregon

Merciful God, in prayer I lift my eyes beyond my own horizons to a world drifting without purpose—one that desperately needs your touch. In the places you position me, let me be your salt, your light, your strength to people who secretly long for your presence.

Cabin, Colorado

Previous pages - Above the Cascade Mountains, Oregon

Lord Jesus, you were unafraid of power and privilege, but you chose to live simply as a carpenter. You loved to visit with Mary, Martha and Lazarus at their kitchen table. You stood beside the woman who was shunned because of her sin. You joined Zacchaeus and his friends for a feast in his home.

You comforted each person searching for light in darkness. Whenever one life faltered, you held out your hand and offered a brand new beginning. I stand amazed that you can see the potential in each one of us—the promise of a whole life surrendered to you through the power of the Holy Spirit.

Short-eared owl, Colorado

Redwoods, Redwood National Park, California

Foxtail grasses and yarrow, Alaska

*P*recious Lord, sometimes days, even weeks can fly by without my acknowledging your presence. Yet I can see where your hand swept over this earth to create the expanse of prairie grasslands, old-growth forests, and the blue brilliance of these Indian summer skies.

Remind me, O God, that I can experience your presence anew in the cocoon's veiled promise or the simple faith of a child's prayer. Grant me the clarity of vision to recognize your hand in each moment of the day.

Vermillion flycatcher, Arizona

September harvest, Montana

White-crowned sparrow, Alaska

*E*ternal God, I yearn to live with such power,

passion, and purpose that my life might be an

instrument of your grace in this needy world.

So I pray for the gift of integrity—to live so

authentically that my character will shine even

with no one watching my steps. I ask for the

gift of a humble heart, offering myself freely

and abundantly, with neither hunger for status,

nor fear of obscurity. Come and journey with

me, gracious Master, as I seek to honor and

serve you.

Snake River and Teton Range, Grand Teton National Park, Wyoming

Mighty God, I invite you to take me atop the soaring mountains of the spirit. Allow me to see, for just a moment, beyond the limits of this world, to sense your vision for your kingdom— and for my own life.

Abba, I know you as the one who heals, the one who holds me close to your heart. You reach out in my moments of deepest need to remind me that I am precious and beloved to you. You find me lonely, broken, despairing and restore me to promising new horizons. You touch the blindness in my soul and make me see afresh. You love me deeply when I cannot face myself.

When my burdens are overwhelming, you gently carry the load on your shoulders. When my doubts are deep, you plant the seed of faith. And when I need the courage to turn around and begin again, your grace leads the way. I worship you, O God, for you alone are the wellspring of all

my hope and strength.

Desert paintbrush, Arches National Park, Utah

Cadillac Mountain, Acadia National Park, Maine

Fall aster and web, Vermont

God of surpassing goodness, guide me to be radiant in your love

and eager for each day's promise. In the majesty of each morning

and the quiet wonder of each evening, I will whisper your praise.

Tioga Pass, Yosemite National Park, California

Dear Jesus, you listened with gentle respect to the woman at the well and to the man who visited you with questions filling his mind. Grant me the ability to be thoughtful in my speaking and loving in my listening. May I be open to change, always willing to seek just solutions to problems.

Compassionate God, if a soft answer turns away anger, help me to choose responses that will heal the wounds of hurt and hatred, leading to a new beginning.

Aspen leaves in first snow, Colorado

Village maple, New York

Glorious God, I pause near a secluded pond, vibrant with the chorus

of autumn's song, as all your creatures hurry to prepare for winter.

In these moments of blessed solitude, teach me to make time to rest

in prayer.

Help me to come to you as I really am—

no masks, no pretensions. I am beaten

and battered by the challenges of life,

wounded and weary from its daily demands.

Gracious God, embrace me in your arms of

love. Help me to remember to rejoice because

you have already won the victory. O Lord,

hear this prayer whispered silently in the

quiet pleading of my heart.

Canada goose, Ohio

Autumn tundra, Alaska

*G*od of all generations, on this sunlit Thanksgiving morn, I feel blessed to be with family, delighting in fall's bountiful harvest. I give thanks for health, hope, and friendship in my life. I turn to you, precious Lord, so grateful that your faithfulness stretches across the heavens and your love spans the farthest reaches of the stars. Yet you reach out to me, calling me by name. You remind me that when I seek you with all my heart, you will find me.

Dear God, I know that you also embrace the ones who do not yet know your love. Minister to each through your grace so that all will know the joy of abiding in you.

Napa Valley grapes, California

Stone barn, Mt. Desert Island, Maine

*E*ver present God, you soar on the winds of time, yet you accompany me to barbecues, my workplace, and along the roadways of my life. On this misty morning, may your Holy Spirit dwell within me, empowering me to remember Jesus' words with every step I take.

Redwoods, Redwood National Park, California

Emma's Creek, Oregon

Winter

Arctic fox, Manitoba

Elk, Yellowstone National Park, Wyoming

*I*delight in the

surprising freedom of

laughter that opens

my heart to your joy,

dear God.

Winter holly, Oregon

Winter barn, Minturn, Colorado

*T*hank you, Everlasting Father, for the return of the wondrous magic of the Christmas

season. I cherish the familiar melodies reminding me of that great Christmas miracle—

when the Lord of the universe came as a baby to lie in the caress of his mother's arms.

O God, before such mystery, I kneel, rejoicing.

Harp seal pup, Gulf of St. Lawrence, Canada (both)

*B*lessed Lord, help me to support others, rejoicing with those who rejoice and weeping with those who weep. I want to be like Jesus, responding with compassion and sensitivity to each person who crosses my path. Open my eyes, O God, so that I can recognize Jesus guiding my every step.

O God of all creation, thank you for the blessing of crystal clear nights when I can ponder the beauty of stars flung across the heavens. I marvel at the sparkle of lights adorning homes, reflecting the joy of the birth of Jesus, the light of the world.

As I find myself immersed in Christmas preparations, I pray for a glimpse of your celestial vision. Help me to recognize the trace of your hand in the angel voices that carol in the most unlikely places. The unexpected kindness and generosity of strangers and friends renews my spirit, reminding me of your unending love for all people.

Holiday cabin, Colorado

Poinsettia, Illinois

*M*ost Holy God, I pray that my mind would be hushed and my

spirit stilled. Then I might hear the brush of angel wings, reminding

me that you have gifted the world with your Son, who is truly

'Emmanuel, God with us'. Precious Lord, the love you offer exceeds

the deepest expression of my longing, for you are far greater than

the human heart. Direct each thought and each effort of my life, so

that my limits will not obscure your love shining through me.

O God of this holy Christmas Eve, in the darkness an infant cries. From the heavens descends a song, "Alleluia, Glory in the highest." On this night of nights, I delight in the glow of Christmas candles, cherish the wonder of pajama-clad cherubs, and give thanks for all the secret shepherds among us.

God of all galaxies, your majesty is revealed in vastness and power, yet you visited this earth in the form of a tiny baby. I rejoice in your gentleness personified in Mary and Joseph's blessed family. This is the time when I believe anew that love is stronger than fear and peace more enduring than anger. The cloak of darkness will never extinguish the light of your glory.

O Lord, as my spirit yields to the spirit of your Son, Jesus, may my Christmas be spent as a gift to those I love. In the candlelight, fill me with glad joy until my own voice exultantly joins with the angel chorus. Jesus Christ is born today. Christ is born to us.

O God of light, on this quiet day I am resting after the pace of the Christmas season. I come before you hoping that the radiance of Christmas will not ebb away, praying that the spirit of compassion will not fade away, and believing that the promise of the manger will be kept alive.

O living Christ, help me to glimpse your presence in mangers and mansions, on crowded roads and on the gloomiest winter day. As you once came to dwell in this world, come now and live fully in me. Be born in me, O Lord. Be born in every part of my being.

Winter barn, Oregon

*S*hepherd of my soul, as I enter into the freshness of a new year, I pray that you will visit me and touch those secret places in my life that most need to change. Some are so deep that they have no name. Some burdens I have carried for such a long time. I offer them to you now, knowing that you are the source of all healing.

Tear down the barriers that keep me from loving others. Root out all hatred and violence from my life. Free me from addiction to any person, thing, or substance so that I might place my full trust in you.

My deepest desire is that you would change my heart, O God, bringing me forgiveness and peace. Then give me the strength to let go and begin afresh.

King penguin, South Georgia Island

Pioneer Ridge, Denali, Alaska

*E*ternal Fashioner of this gift of evening peace, I enter your presence with whispers of praise welling up from deep within me. My heart awakens anew when I view the masterpiece of a winter night. I give thanks for the stars piercing the midnight sky and the snow twinkling like diamond dust, blanketing the landscape.

Grant me the gift of a calmed spirit, as you teach me the discipline of quieting my soul by your stilled stream. The clamor of my noisy mind, overfilled with the urgent demands of a busy life, can overwhelm the important priorities in my home. Let my mind pause long enough to receive the power of your Word, "Peace, be still."

Icy Ponderosa pine, Oregon

Carolyn's Crown Natural Area, Cascade Mountains, Oregon

*O*God of my life, I thank you that I am alive—

alive in this beautiful world, alive on this magnificent day.

Winter walk, Colorado

O God of hope, for just a moment I pause, wholly attentive to you. Facing a complex, confusing decision, I pray that you will enable me to make the right choice and then rest in your wisdom. I yearn for a closer walk with you, so teach me to trust you with abandon. Minister to the deepest cries of my heart, O Lord, so that I can go forth with a renewed mind, a revived confidence, and a rested soul.

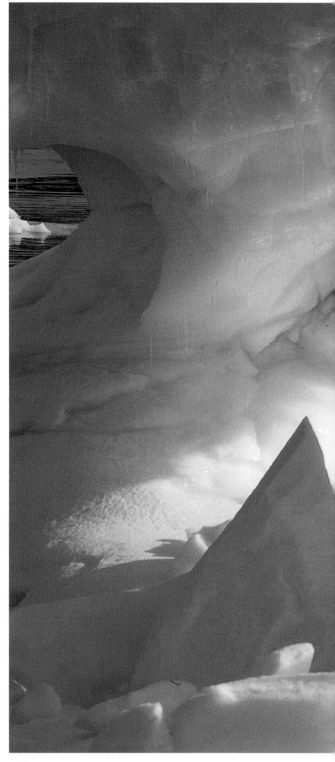

Iceberg cave, Antarctica

Sanibel Island shells, Florida

Wherever I am in this new year, O Lord, help me to draw strength from prayer, so that I would know the serenity and purpose of a life devoted to you. Fill me with the light of your Holy Spirit, that Christ might shine in me always.

M ighty God, weave me into the tapestry of people ready to impact our worlds with your love. Bind us together by the power of Jesus—breathing passion and purpose into lives ready to serve.

Crab pots, Depot Bay, Oregon

Benediction

Mt. Shuksan, Washington

O Lord, go before me to prepare the way, walk behind me to be my protection, and stand beside me to be my most faithful friend.

Biblical Notes

Nauset Beach, Massachusetts
Previous pages - Mesa Arch sunrise, Canyonlands National Park, Utah

SPRING

SUMMER

Taconic Range, Vermont

R

Reflection, 59
Rejoice, 22, 39, 98, 109, 111
Renewal, 26, 112, 126
Rest, 65, 118, 126

S

Seeker, 53, 85, 100
Service, 47, 59, 75, 83, 89, 128, 130
Sin, 33
Sorrow, 33, 39, 111
Soul, 25, 35, 39, 42, 47, 61, 79, 92, 122, 126
Spirit, 25, 53, 69, 91, 112, 115, 116, 118, 122
(see also Holy Spirit)
Spring, 25, 26, 35, 39
Strength, 59, 65, 72, 79, 83, 92, 121, 128
Summer, 56, 69, 87
Support for others, 111
Surrender, 85

T

Teachers, 80
Thanksgiving, 100
Time, 29, 31, 56, 80, 98, 102, 116, 121
Trust in God, 26, 42, 44, 47, 61, 67, 72, 121, 126

V

Vacation, 65
Victory, 33, 98
Violence, 121
Vision, 87, 91, 112

W

Walk with God, 47, 89, 126, 135
Weakness, 55
Winter, 98, 122
Wisdom, 41, 72, 126
Witness to others, 79, 83
Woman at well, 97
World, 26, 59, 62, 83, 87, 89, 91, 115, 125, 130
Worries, 31, 39

Y

Youth, 80

Z

Zacchaeus, 85

Radiant
River Press

Radiant River Press, 1258 Willowgate Lane, St. Charles, IL 60174
www.radiantriverpress.com

Name: _____

Address: _____

City: _____ State: _____ Zip: _____

Phone: (_____) _____ Email address: _____

Please send the following books to my home address above:

Quantity	Price for one $34.95	Book price
_____		_____

Add 6.5% sales tax for books shipped to Illinois ($2.27 each)   _____

Shipping and handling: Add $5 for first book and $3 for each additional book   _____

Please send the following books as a gift to:

Name: _____

Address: _____

City: _____ State: _____ Zip: _____

Quantity	Price for one $34.95	Total price
_____		_____

Add 6.5% sales tax for books shipped to Illinois ($2.27each)   _____

Shipping and handling: Add $5 for first book and $3 for each additional book   _____

Add $5 for gift wrap and card: _____

Note for card (please print):

TOTAL PAYMENT ENCLOSED $ _____
Please make check payable to Radiant River Press.
For credit card orders call JupiterFIRST Church at 561-747-8340 or e-mail them at jupiterfirst@aol.com.
Attach extra sheets for additional orders to different addresses.

Call us at 1-866-259-7080 or e-mail us at info@radiantriverpress.com with any questions.
Thank you very much for your order.